# MUSIC FROM THE MOTION PICTURE SOUNDTRACK

ISBN 978-1-4584-2357-3

HAL•LEONARD®
CORPORATION

7777 W. BLUEMOUND RD. P.O. BOX 13819 MILWAUKEE, WI 53213

In Australia Contact:
**Hal Leonard Australia Pty. Ltd.**
4 Lentara Court
Cheltenham, Victoria, 3192 Australia
Email: ausadmin@halleonard.com.au

Visit Hal Leonard Online at
**www.halleonard.com**

# THE ARTIST OUVERTURE

Composed by LUDOVIC BOURCE

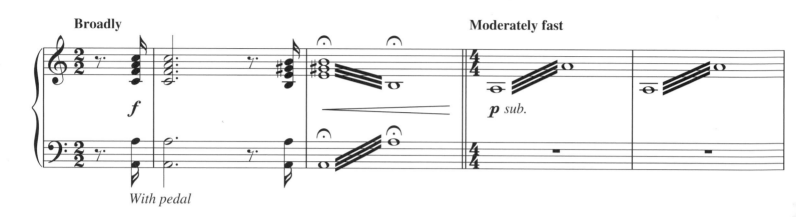

# GEORGE VALENTIN

Composed by LUDOVIC BOURCE

**Bright Swing**

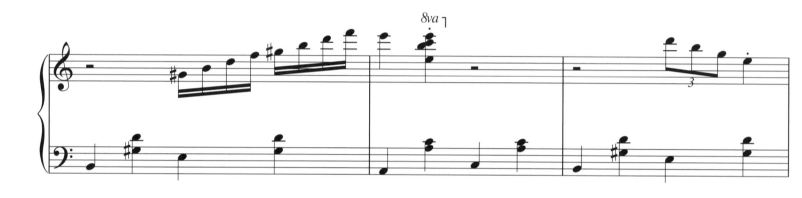

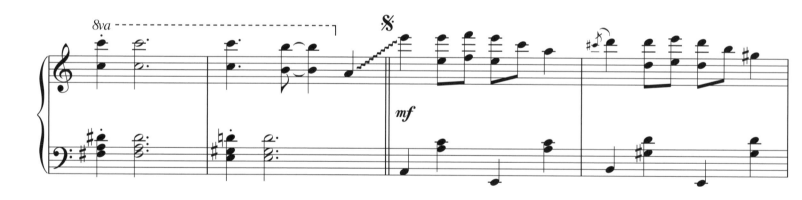

To Coda

**Play 4 times**

*mp*  *dim. poco a poco*

**D.S. al Coda**

*mp*

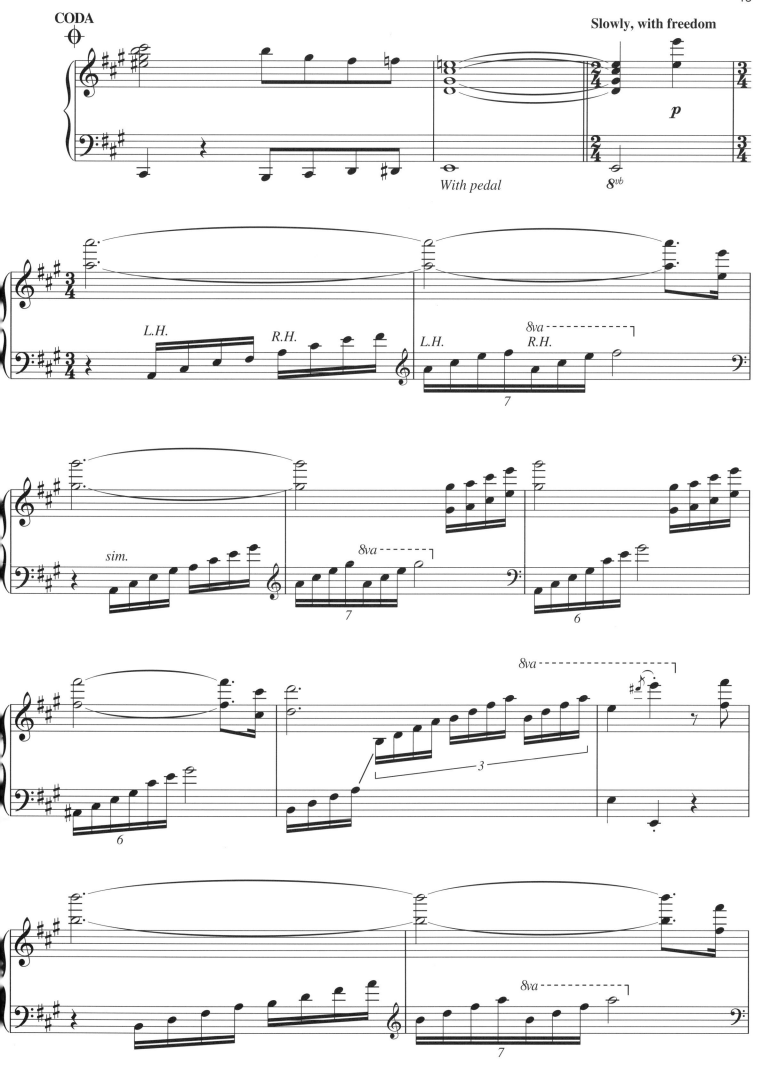

**Easy Swing**

*mp*

*rit.*

*Segue to "Pretty Peppy"*

# PRETTY PEPPY

Composed by LUDOVIC BOURCE

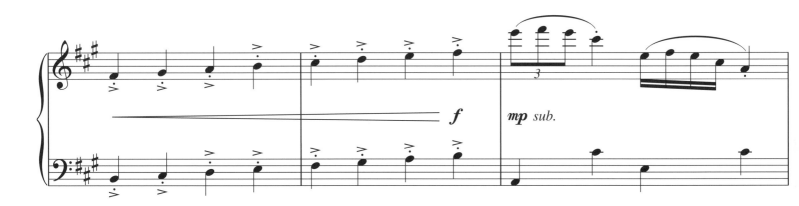

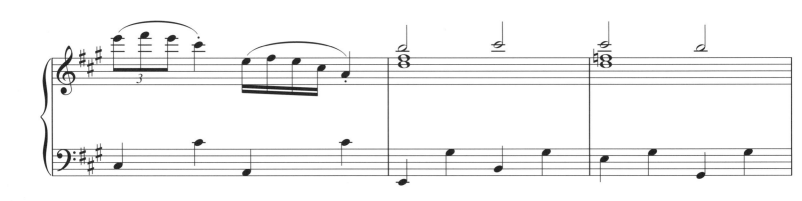

*Segue to "At the Kinograph Studios"*

# AT THE KINOGRAPH STUDIOS

Composed by LUDOVIC BOURCE

**Tempo I**

*Segue to "Fantaisie d'amor"*

# FANTAISIE D'AMOR

Composed by LUDOVIC BOURCE

**Vivacious Swing**

With pedal

*Segue to "Waltz for Peppy"*

# WALTZ FOR PEPPY

Composed by LUDOVIC BOURCE

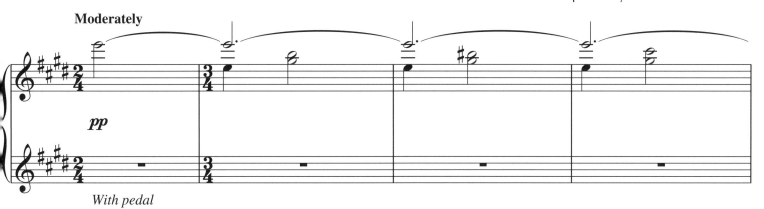

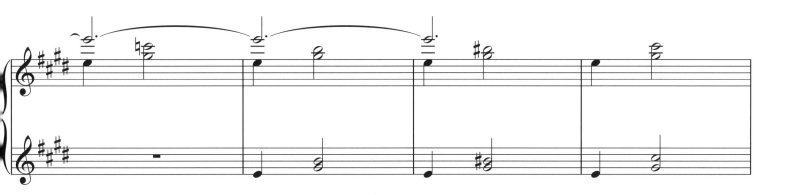

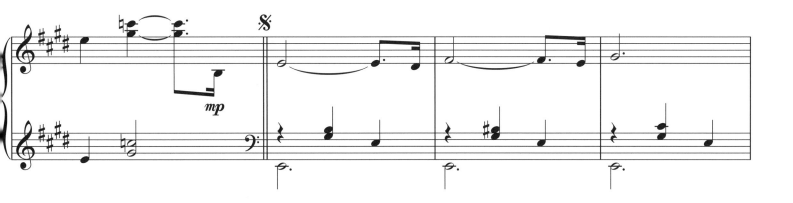

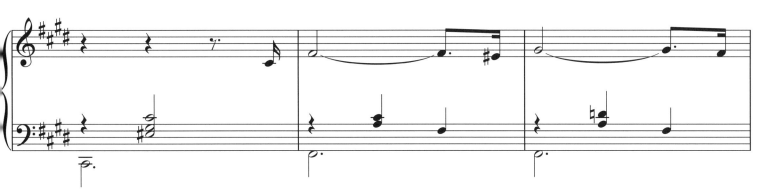

*a tempo*

*mf*

(R.H.)

**D.S. al Coda**

*mp*

42

CODA

Slowly, with freedom

# COMME UNE ROSÉE DE LARMES

Composed by LUDOVIC BOURCE

**Slowly**

*With pedal*

**With more motion**

# 1931

Composed by LUDOVIC BOURCE

**Moderately slow, languid**

**p**

*sim.*

*With pedal*

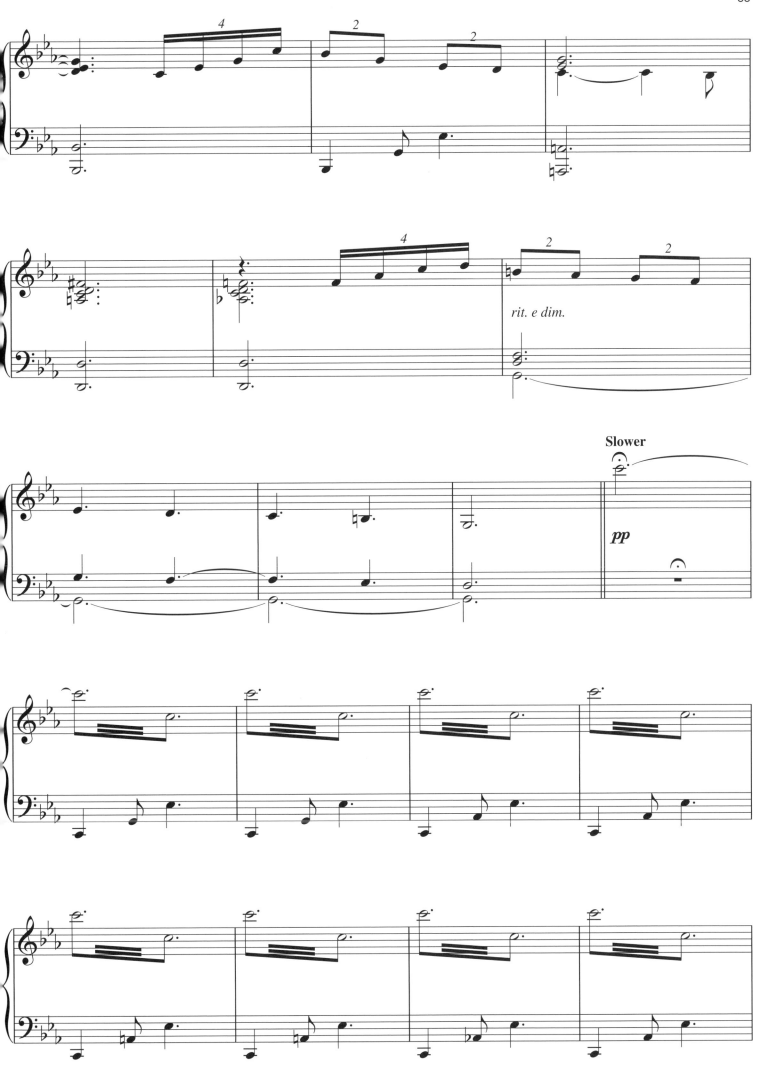

# PEPPY AND GEORGE

Composed by LUDOVIC BOURCE

**Bright Swing**